Greetings from Lowestoft
By
Malcolm White

Coastal and Maritime Heritage Series

2001

INFORMATION

Published by	Malcolm R. White	Printed by	Micropress Printers Ltd.
	71 Beeching Drive		27 Norwich Road
	Lowestoft		Halesworth
	NR32 4TB		IP19 8BX
	England, UK		England, UK

First Published   November 2001   ISBN 0 9532485 5 0

Please Note
Every effort has been made to ensure the information in this book is accurate. For this reason, official documentation backed up by various research works, and local records have been consulted for factual support. However, when considering such a complex, variable and historical subject, with some material attributable to other parties, 100% accuracy cannot be guaranteed.

Front Cover Photograph
This novel and futuristic postcard from before the First World War, shows a family flying in and about to land on the South Pier at the end of their journey. Part of the message on the card is " Got here at 6.45. Much headwind! "
This card was published by J. J. Webb, The Bridge , Lowestoft

Title Page Photograph
A fine 1903 view looking south from the Royal Plain. The Esplanade and the Royal Hotel, seen on the immediate right, were part of Sir Morton Peto's plan in the mid 1800s to establish a new town south of the harbour, and hence create South Lowestoft.

Opposite Page Photograph
The town of Lowestoft as seen in 1790, with buildings associated with the fishing and other sea trades on the land under the cliff, and the hanging gardens of the many grand houses on the cliff top. Visible on the left, is the tower of the low light, a lighthouse positioned on the beach, which could easily be moved. This wooden structure was replaced in 1867 by a tubular steel lighthouse, again easily moveable. The reason for the low light being made portable was that it could be physically shifted to indicate any movement of the dangerous offshore shoals, and together with the highlight on the cliffs, give mariners an accurate indication of the safe channel through these shoals. The low light was taken out of service in 1923.

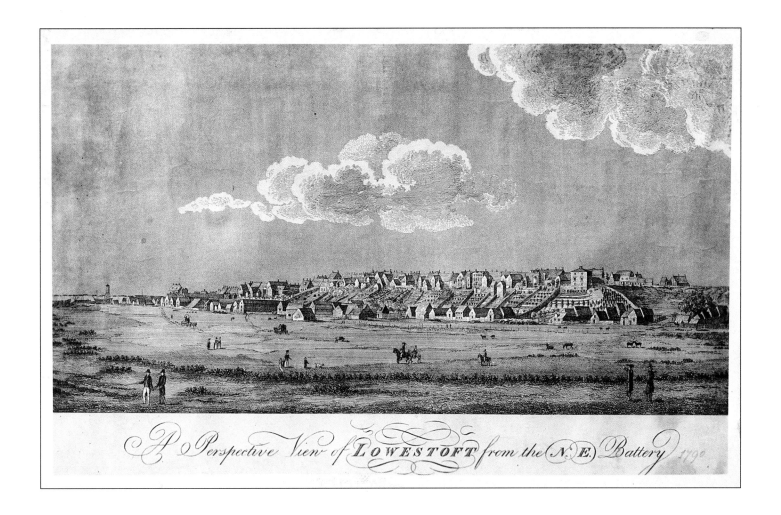

A Perspective View of LOWESTOFT from the (N.E.) Battery 1790

CONTENTS

ACKNOWLEDGEMENTS

Much appreciated has been the support and assistance from a number of kind and generous people during the preparation of this book, and in particular, Mr. Stuart Jones BA, Mr. Peter Killby and Mr. David White. Stuart has provided editorial support for all six titles in the series, and Peter and David have supplied many of the postcards and photographs seen in this book.

PHOTOGRAPHIC OWNERSHIP AND COPYRIGHT

Other books in the Coastal and Maritime Series by Malcolm White.........

DOWN THE HARBOUR 1955-1995
40 years of fishing vessels, owners, the harbour and shipyards at Lowestoft   ISBN 09532485 0 X
A CENTURY OF FISHING
Fishing from Great Yarmouth and Lowestoft   ISBN 09532485 1 8
FISHING WITH DIVERSITY
A portrait of the Colne Group of Lowestoft   ISBN 09532485 2 6
CROWNIES OF LOWESTOFT
The steam trawler fleet of Consolidated Fisheries   ISBN 09532485 3 4
DRIFTING, TRAWLING & SHIPPING
A portrait of Small & Co. (Lowestoft) Ltd.   ISBN 09532485 4 2

A view from the "Space Tower", South Pier Pavilion 1957.

In the early 1900s, a tram heads north up London Road North and away from the junction with Suffolk Road and Denmark Road. On the left is the *Suffolk Hotel*, built in 1873 which replaced an earlier hotel of the same name. After demolition of this fine Trust House establishment in late 1971, Liptons supermarket was built there. Upon closure of the supermarket in 1983, the site was acquired for the present MacDonald's fast food restaurant.

5

The Esplanade looking north from what is now the car park opposite the Claremont Pier. This early 1900s view shows a litter free and clean sea front with everybody smartly dressed, bathing machines on the beach, a temporary concert party stage and seating area, and a goat cart conveying a little girl, no doubt having a lovely time. In the background, can be seen the elegant and very popular South Pier Pavilion, completed in 1891 and demolished in 1954.

Introduction

Over the years, a large number of books have been written about Lowestoft and the surrounding area. Many of these have repeated, in various forms, the history of the town, and in some cases featured many of the same photographs. This book is unusual in that it portrays the town as holidaymakers, visitors, and others, such as relations and friends at home, would see and perhaps remember the area. We take a photographic journey though bygone Lowestoft starting at the north end of the town, and view some greatly missed and much loved buildings. Many of these were demolished in recent years due to "progressive development", a common factor of modern Lowestoft life. It is intended that the pictures and their captions tell the story rather than long chapters of text, and that the format will bring back many happy memories, and also thoughts of carefree, relaxing and stress free days spent in and around Lowestoft, the town that for generations was portrayed as **Where Broadland meets the Sea**.

Malcolm White
Lowestoft
November 2001

After a heavy snowfall at Lowestoft in the early 1900s

The yacht club was formed in 1859 as the
Norfolk and Suffolk Yacht Club and
established a headquarters at Lowestoft. In
1885 it had the use of a clubhouse, and in
1898, the club received a warrant, entitling
it to add the prefix " Royal " to the club
name. The clubhouse seen here was built
in 1903, opening on the 11ᵗʰ July of that year.
The original clubhouse was moved to the
Crown Meadow football ground for use as a
sports pavilion. This scene shows the
Lowestoft Regatta before the First World War.

8

Foreword

The sending of postcards whilst away from home has traditionally been a way of remembering those in far away places, and a special way of passing on greetings to them. Whilst on holiday, or when just passing as a tourist, photographs have traditionally been taken to help capture a time, when for a brief period we get away from the normal every day routine of life.

Lowestoft has been attracting visitors for many hundreds of years, indeed some of the first were unwelcome invaders from other lands. A notable visitor in 1643 was Oliver Cromwell, who came together with over a thousand of his troops to sort out the Royalist element in the town. In 1736, King George II arrived in Lowestoft after a stormy crossing from the Continent. Later during the same century, visitors included the Duke of Gloucester and Prince William of Gloucester. During the 17th century, the equivalent of the present day tourist and holiday trade started to develop. The town at that time was centred on the High Street area, with fishing and agriculture the main occupations. This was well before the harbour had been constructed, or any development had taken place in the area immediately south of Lake Lothing. By the end of 18th century, Lowestoft was very much a fashionable resort, popular with the gentry and well to do. A well-known aspect of this period was the manufacture of the noted Lowestoft Porcelain, the clay for which was obtained locally. This short-lived industry produced some very much sought after and fine pieces between 1757 and around the end of the 18th century, when the factory closed. During 1823, Lowestoft was described as "having the noblest and most beautiful appearance of any town upon the east coast. Its shore is safe having an easy declivity into the water, with a fine pebbly bottom; here are good bathing machines and this place is much resorted to in the bathing season". The population at that time was 3675 persons, made up of 1711 males and 1964 females. By 1901, the population had risen to 29,850, of which just over 12,000 were in full time work in the town.

The harbour, opened on the 10th August 1831, was initially not very successful. Samuel Morton Peto later improved it, by adding longer outer North and South Piers. He went on to build the first railway line, which would connect Lowestoft with the rest of the country, and advanced the development of the area south of the harbour. Here many fine outstanding buildings and terraces were constructed, some of which have unfortunately since been demolished. The building of the railway meant that many more visitors could come to Lowestoft; and substantially increased the popularity of this most easterly resort. Other railway lines followed and development continued in both halves of the town, with many major amenities being opened and substantial buildings being constructed. Several holiday camps were established near Lowestoft during the early 20th century and these, together with an increasing number of hotels and boarding houses provided the necessary accommodation required by the rapidly increasing number of visitors to the resort and the surrounding area. Lowestoft was well on the way to becoming a popular and important seaside resort much loved by thousands of residents and visitors.

During the 19th and 20th century, a strong diverse industrial base developed in and around the town. This included the traditional fishing industry, tourism, railway engineering, shipbuilding, bus, coach and motorcar construction, electronics, food processing, the manufacture of artist materials, shoes, electrical cables and switchgear, and artificial pearls. Most of these have now disappeared from the local scene. The harbour with the fish market, marine engineering workshops, many port-based businesses, and at one time numerous important railway works and yards have been a major asset to the town, and consistently popular with the sightseer, holiday maker and tourist. In recent years the Lowestoft area has seen the building of a number of large housing estates. These are continuing to be built, to the north, west and south of the town. Today, due to this continued urban sprawl, Lowestoft appears joined to some of its former neighbouring villages and towns with little, if any undeveloped land remaining. The attraction of the Lowestoft and Oulton Broad area remains strong for the new resident, some second homeowners, the tourist and holidaymaker.

The humble greetings postcard remains the first choice for many, when remembering family and friends whilst away from home, even in this age of the E-mail, Internet, mobile phone, information technology and text messaging.

The Warren House, north beach and dunes as seen in the early 1900s. The Warren House was actually a number of dwellings, located close to a spring, and for many years was associated with the manufacture of Lowestoft Porcelain. One of Lowestoft's famous Scores, Grene or Green Score was in this vicinity.

186. LOWESTOFT. 'MID FURZE & HEATHER.

Bus No 4. of the Lowestoft Corporation fleet, a twenty three seater Guy Arab type BB is seen climbing Links Road. It is working the Summer only sea wall service, which for part of the route, ran along the north sea wall. This bus route was introduced, and the road built in the late 1920s. Part of the extensive golf course that once existed in the north denes and beach area is in the background.

A view of the North Denes, before Links Road was constructed. An extensive part of the area seen in in this view was in use for many years as a golf course.

THE DENES, LOWESTOFT.

An unusual print from around 1900 showing the beach in the vicinity of the present day North Denes Caravan Site. The dress is typical of the period for a day on the beach. A strong easterly breeze is blowing, in this afternoon scene.
It would be unusual to find so many people on the north beach in the 21st century .

Development of the North Denes was rapid during the 1920s and 1930s. The Denes Oval recreation ground was established in 1924-25, catering for tennis, golf and cricket. This area had previously been used for allotment gardens. This comprehensive scene also shows the Sparrow's Nest greenhouses, the popular café in the former golf club buildings, a Corporation bus working the amended sea wall service, and the swimming pool and model yacht pond, both in top right of the photograph

The Children's Play Ground, North Lowestoft.

There has been two model yacht ponds situated on the Denes. This is the second of the two which was situated in the children's playground. Behind the adjacent Denes Oval can be seen the cliffs and the Gunton Cliff Esplanade.

A fine view of the Lowestoft Swimming Pool in the 1930s. This pool, together with the model yacht pond, was later filled in and now forms part of the council run North Denes Caravan Site.

IN THE PARK, LOWESTOFT.

In 1874, Belle Vue Park opened on land which had previously been an area of rough ground called North End Common. The cleverly designed layout, gives the impression of a much larger area than it really is. Prominent features of the park were the refreshment pavilion and bandstand, and the weather monitoring station. In this charming scene of elegance and relaxation, just prior to the First World War, the tables are set out ready for afternoon tea, and ladies and gentlemen are seated adjacent to the pavilion. This is now the location of the Royal Naval Patrol Service Memorial.

This scene was recorded in the early 1920s and shows another prominent feature of the park, the Ravine Bridge. This structure was opened on the 29th August 1887. It formed a direct link between the park and the North Parade and Gunton Cliff area, at that time subject to housing development. The bridge was the gift of the town's first mayor, Alderman William Youngman, and commemorates the Jubilee of Queen Victoria. The two large houses on the right were built in the 1860s.

Ravine Bridge with Parade, Lowestoft.

RAVINE BRIDGE & PARK, LOWESTOFT.

An unusual and delightful view across The Ravine, Belle Vue Park, Sparrow's Nest Park and Denes. The white post visible amongst the trees on the right, was associated with the weather station

Adjacent to the Belle Vue Park, is the 6.9 acre Sparrow's Nest Park, the name being derived from the 19th century owner of the park, Mr. Robert Sparrow, who used the large house in the grounds, as a summer home. Mr. Sparrow of Worlingham Hall, together with the Reverend Frances Bowness, Rector of Gunton, set up a fund in 1800 to build the first lifeboat for Lowestoft. Unfortunately the boat itself was not liked by those meant to crew her, and saw little service. It was later rejected. Sparrow's Nest has had a number of owners including Sir Edward Hall Alderson, the Rev. Dr. William Whewell who used the name of Clyffe Cottage, Belle Vue Park, for the house, and Mr. Joseph Davey who left the property to his daughter Margaret. In 1897, the property was auctioned, the eventual owner being Lowestoft Corporation, who went on to name the park Sparrow's Nest. In the 20th century, the venue became involved in entertainment, with concert parties, circus acts and variety, being presented by Mr. Frank Stebbings. Later, the Council took over and presented these in a marquee, and eventually in the greatly missed Sparrow's Nest Pavilion Theatre. This much loved building was opened in 1913 and improved in 1933. It was demolished in 1991. During the Second World War, the park and buildings were taken over for military use and became Pembroke X and later HMS Europa, the Central Depot of the Royal Naval Patrol Service.

Top Right - A peaceful scene recorded in the Sparrow's Nest Park before the First World War. In the early 1960s, most of the remaining parts of the original house were demolished.

Bottom Right - Another view from before the First World War. Looking across the lawn to the present location of the shell bandstand. A popular feature of the gardens in the mid 20th century was Robbie playing the mighty organ.

An unusual and quite historic scene inside the Sparrow's Nest Theatre. Few quality photographs have been preserved showing a full audience inside the theatre. The date is the 20th March 1974, and the ladies of the Women's Institute are obviously enjoying themselves.

The popular Sparrow's Nest Theatre which was demolished in 1991. Many well known stars of stage, screen and television appeared at this theatre, in addition to the popular summer season shows, such as *Dazzle* and *Starlight Rendezvous*. For a great many years this theatre was advertised as "The Showpiece Of The East Coast".

At first, the location of this 1890s scene may seem unfamiliar. However, the presence of two well-known present day buildings on the right, may help to identify the location. The white building in the distance is the lighthouse or Highlight, and the building nearest to the camera on the right, is Arnold House, at the end of St. Margaret's Road. The buildings on the left of this photograph, were demolished over 100 years ago, the nearest of which is *The Three Herrings* public house.

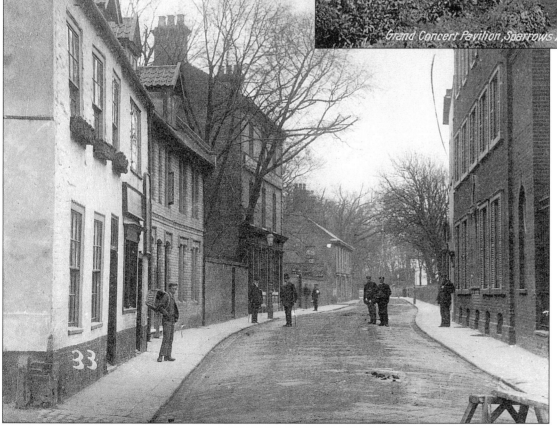

After representation by various ship owners, merchants and others, to the Corporation of Trinity House, concerning the loss of ships and cargoes on the sandbanks and shoals off the town, it was proposed that two light towers or beacons be located at Lowestoft. In 1609, these candlelights were positioned in the beach area at the foot of the cliff. It was not until 1676 that one of them, the Highlight, was positioned on the cliff top. The other beacon, the Lowlight remained on the beach and consisted of a wooden framed moveable tower. It was discontinued in 1706, but re-established in 1730, and rebuilt a number of times. On the last occasion in 1867, it was replaced by a tower of tubular steel. In August 1923, the Lowlight was considered surplus to requirements, and taken out of service.

Below - Viewed from the Denes, the top of the Highlight can be seen just above the trees. The picturesque cottages at the bottom of Lighthouse Score backed on to the Sparrow's Nest Park and were demolished in 1938, to make way for modern council houses. In the foreground can be seen posts, nets, and ropes associated with the herring fishing.

Above – The 1867 built steel Lowlight.

18

84241. Convalscent Home. Lowestoft.

This building, which stands opposite Belle Vue Park and the Highlight, was originally in use as the Boys National School. In 1877, the school moved to different premises and the building, together with the extensive gardens became the Lowestoft Convalescent Home. Enlarged in 1882, it served as a home for most of the 20th century.

It is seen here before the First World War, during which the building suffered extensive shell damage in the 1916 bombardment of the town by the German Navy.

Eventually, the Home closed and was sold. The building became Abigail Court, and the grounds were used for the building of Trinity Methodist Church, and also the High Street Surgery.

The present Lowestoft Lighthouse or Highlight, adjoins the Sparrow's Nest Park. This view from the 1920s shows a number of features of the period, including the overhead wires and rails of the tramway system, the First World War tank, a sign indicating the way to the swimming pool and fine columns marking the entrance to the Sparrow's Nest Park. Just visible is a "Lighthouse Open" sign hanging on the lighthouse wall.

A coal fired light tower was erected in 1676 on the site of the present lighthouse. In 1778, the coal fire was replaced by oil lamps and a reflector. Many repairs, modifications and improvements were carried out on the light and tower over the years, including the use of vaporised oil lamps and various lenses. During 1873, the present tower was built, with the light initially consisting of paraffin burners and the latest optical system. Conversion to electricity took place in 1936, and the lighthouse became unmanned in 1975.

HIGH LIGHTHOUSE, LOWESTOFT

Extensive demolition and rebuilding took place in the High Street in the late 1800s and early 1900s. This was due to the need to widen the road. Most of the properties on the west side were set back, including the Town Hall. This can be seen here in the late 1880s on the left, and behind the *Red Lion* public house.

A postcard sent in 1904 showing tramcar No. 11 heading south down the High Street, past the reconstructed Town Hall. A gentleman in uniform has just hailed the tram. Thankfully much of the property in this view remains today, but unfortunately, some totally out of place development, has been allowed to intrude

High Street, Lowestoft

Valentines Series

An interesting early view of the High Street before the demolition of the west side properties. At that time, the Town Hall had public houses on either side, one of which is just visible on the left. The narrow nature of the street is quite evident from this postcard.

It appears that little has changed in the High Street since the 1920s, when this card was published. However, the types of shop have changed, and no longer do we have grocers, sweetshops, newsagents and greengrocers supplying everyday needs.

A 1920s view of part of the Old Market Plain, with some of the residents, and customers of the *Black Swan* public house lined up for the photographer. During the mid 1960s all this property was demolished to make way for new roads and other development.

An area which has seen many changes is the Triangle. The layout and road structure has been changed a number of times since this photograph was taken in the early part of the 20th century.

Old Nelson Street was a relatively minor road in the 1920s. With a park at the bottom on Battery Green, the location was an area of of peace and tranquillity. This was to change in the late 1970s and early 1980s, when all property of the east side of the road was demolished to make way for the southbound A12 trunk road. This photograph was taken from what is now the centre of a large traffic roundabout.

LOWESTOFT. THE PICKLING PLOTS. 207

Not far from Old Nelson Street was an area known as the Pickling Plots. These were a hive of activity during the autumn home fishing. It was here that the majority of the herring landed at Lowestoft were processed by Scotch fisher girls. For much of the year however, they were deserted. In this view, barrels are stored awaiting the start of the season, and nets can be seen hanging out drying in the background. These nets would been immersed in a hot solution of a substance known as cutch in the net store copper, in order to preserve them. In the centre of the postcard, on the cliffs can be seen the Lighthouse, still known to many as the Highlight.

At one time it seemed that the majority of the townsfolk were involved in one way or another, with the arrival of the vast herring shoals in the southern North Sea during the autumn months. A large fleet of local and visiting Scottish herring drifters, worked out of Lowestoft during this period and landed vast amounts of fish on the market. Photographs and postcards of this period are very popular both for locals, tourists and holidaymakers.

The postcard on the right shows the Scottish herring drifter *BF148 J. & M. Main* leaving port with several other drifters. She was built in 1913 at Great Yarmouth and was owned by Mr. W. Donaldson of Portknockie. Sights such as this, could be seen well into the 1950s. At that time, the fleet comprised of a mixture of diesel and steam powered vessels.

DRIFTERS LEAVING HARBOUR, LOWESTOFT (L.101)

Originally referred to as the Herring Basin, the Waveney Dock was for many years a scene of hectic activity, as seen here, during the herring season. Many steam herring drifters are seen in the dock, as they land their catches. After landing, and taking on ice, coal, and other supplies, they would soon be heading out to sea again for the herring grounds. With falling catches and rising costs, the last herring drifter ceased work and was sold in 1968. Scenes such as this would never be seen again.

Lowestoft Herring and Mackerel Market in about 1903. This was situated adjacent to the Waveney Dock and opened with the dock on 1st October 1883. Built by the Great Eastern Railway it was complete with spandrels bearing the initials GER, and gave the impression of a large railway station.

Lowestoft Fishing Industry.– Pickling Herrings.

The Scottish fisher girls followed the herring drifter fleet from the Scottish ports, down the east coast to Lowestoft and Yarmouth. Their work was to gut and pack the herring in barrels. On the left, they can be seen packing herring in barrels, and on the right, filling the barrels with brine prior to sealing. They would have earlier been employed on gutting the fish. Large numbers of barrels, full of herring, were exported.

"A Good Breeze" Lowestoft.

S.Y. AGATHA. R.Y.C.

Above – Large numbers of swans were a feature of the harbour for many years. They were usually found near the outfall of the two canning factories, where there was food. This family has ventured into the Trawl Dock where they are being fed near the trawler *Helping Hand.* Leaving for sea is the steam trawler *Shamrock.*

Top Right - The sailing trawler or "smack" *LT291 Gladiolus*, built in 1901 at Rye, leaves port with two other smacks for the fishing grounds. She was owned by Arthur Evans, and left Lowestoft in 1936 after being sold to Norway.

Bottom Right - Typical of many superb steam yachts of the period, this scene from 1905 shows the *Agatha* in the Yacht Basin. Prominent is the South Pier Pavilion, this impressive structure was completed in 1891, and replaced the reading rooms destroyed by fire in 1885.

LOWESTOFT. SWING BRIDGE. (110.)

With the Swing Bridge open, the smack *LT956 George Borrow* makes her way into the channel, and the Outer Harbour. A particularly clear view can be obtained of the unusual and intricate mechanism required to enable the overhead tramway wires to cross the bridge, and remain continuous once the bridge is back in the normal position. This high quality postcard was published by A. Crisp & Son of 22 High Street, Lowestoft, just before the First World War.

Some postcards were used as Christmas Greeting Cards, such as this view of the harbour mouth. The larger vessels are, from left to right, the pleasure steamer *Lord Roberts*, a sailing trawler leaving the harbour, the private lifeboat *Carolina Hamilton*, and at sea on the right, one of the Lowestoft paddle tugs.

Entrance to Harbour, Lowestoft.

Taken from an original glass plate negative, this print shows a typical event off the South Pier during the autumn home fishing in the 1920s. The paddle tug *Despatch*, sounding a warning blast on her whistle, is about to enter the harbour, as a sailing trawler leaves for the fishing grounds. Following the tug are two steam herring drifters. The *Despatch* was built in 1875 at Poplar, lengthened in 1876, and had a new boiler in 1907. She was sold for scrapping in 1936.

LOWESTOFT. THE OUTER HARBOUR. 34

What must be one of the most comprehensive views to be recorded on one postcard can be seen here. This was taken from the Mount, a look out tower, situated on the fish market. Truly an amazing scene of activity and pictorial delight, the many aspects include the visiting fishery protection cruiser, the dredger working in the Trawl Dock, a sailing trawler about to leave for the fishing grounds and the tug *Lowestoft* in the Yacht Basin. The background includes the Royal Hotel, Claremont Pier together with the landing stage at the end, the Esplanade with many of the villas, and the South Pier, complete with pavilion and bandstand.

PIER REGATTA DAY LOWESTOFT.

Many people believe that the recent annual air shows, are the only occasions, when vast crowds have flocked to the sea front area. However, large crowds are seen here just before First World War for the Lowestoft Regatta.

The pavilion on the South Pier was demolished in 1954. Despite being replaced by a new Pavilion, many people still felt a strong affection for the old building.

THE HARBOUR, LOWESTOFT.

Until the late 20th century, pleasure steamers and other similar craft, had enjoyed a long association with Lowestoft.

This excellent view, taken from the old pavilion in 1909, shows a Great Yarmouth based paddle steamer, disembarking her many passengers for them to spend a few hours in Lowestoft, before returning them to Yarmouth. The Great Yarmouth Steam Tug Co. Ltd. ran these popular trips, costing 1s 3d (6 new pence), twice daily in season. At one time, they also ran excursions from Great Yarmouth to Southwold.

The *Lowestoft Belle* was a popular river steamer. She was built in 1906 by Fellows at Great Yarmouth, and was powered by a 22hp compound steam engine. This fine view of her was recorded in 1913. The *Lowestoft Belle* was owned by Sterry's River Trips.

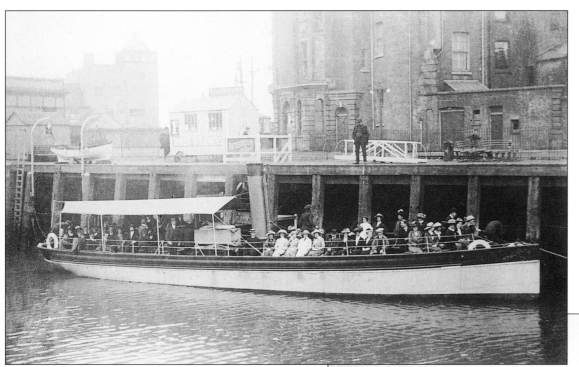

Another river steamer running pleasure trips from Lowestoft was the *Atalanta*. She is seen at the embarkation point used for many years, by different vessels, adjacent to the swing bridge. One of the last pleasure cruisers to use this location for river trips was the famous former lifeboat *Elizabeth Simpson*, skippered by Captain W. Beale. Details of the popular trips made by this 19th century vessel are to be found on the inside of the back cover

An unusual view of the entrance to the harbour, and one that is no longer possible to obtain. The trawler entering port on return from a fishing trip is *LT155 Filby Queen*. This location was traditionally popular with photographers and anglers. It could be quite dangerous walking on the planks, which were quite slippery. Should one fall there was a considerable drop into surging water and slippery rocks beneath.

Ships of the Fishery Protection Squadron have long been visitors to Lowestoft, and were often open to the public when in port. These vessels could usually be found in the Yacht Basin, which is where we find the Algerine Class minesweeper *H.M.S. Welcome* in the early 1950s. At one time the squadron had a base at Lowestoft. Fishery protection work can be traced back to 1379.

Another harbour view from the 1950s, and one which would have been familiar to locals and holiday makers. A Lowestoft fishing vessel, in this case the drifter/trawler *LT387 Young Duke*, is seen heading for the pier heads and sea. She was built in 1953 by the Lowestoft shipbuilder Richards Ironworks.

London Road North in 1928 appears clean and well kept as a tram heads north. The tramway system would only have a few years left before closure. The last tram ran in May 1931.

Woolworth's store on the left proclaims they are the "3d and 6d Store", and Mr. Carr wishes it to be known that he is the "The Value Draper".

29 London Road, Lowestoft

London Road, Lowestoft   5417.

By 1911, buildings that we recognise today had started to appear in London Road North including the Post Office. The trees help to project a park like and more leisurely atmosphere to the shopping area. These would soon be cut down to allow further development to take place.

As well as being close to Lowestoft Central railway station, Station Square was for many years, the location of several different bus stops used by Lowestoft Corporation and Eastern Counties buses, and their predecessors. A group of Lowestoft Corporation busmen gather on the island, which was once a feature of the square, for photographer Mr John Wells in the early 1950s. From left to right, they are Messrs. Boon, not known, D. Martin, J. Hart, not known, L. Vallace, J. Smith, G. Keys, Wright and A. Wright.

Right - For many years a branch of the London and Provincial Bank, this building is perhaps best known as the furniture department of Tuttle's, and later Debenham's departmental store. Debenham's closed the store in 1981, and it has since been divided into small shop units.

The building was the scene of a serious fire in July 1964, when the tower and roof of the building were destroyed. It is at present in use as a pizza restaurant. The date of the photograph is 1911.

Below – The Suffolk Hotel, built in 1873, presents an imposing image in this 1920s view. At the end of 1971, work started to demolish the building. At present the site is occupied by a fast food restaurant and offices. The hotel of 50 bedrooms, had a large dining room with separate tables, a large billiard room, commercial room, smoking lounges and drawing rooms. Just across the road from the railway station, it was normal for hotel porters to meet guests at the station and carry their luggage to their hotel room.

Suffolk Hotel, Lowestoft.

The town has had a number of bridges across the Inner Harbour entrance, some of which have been temporary. The original swing bridge of 1830 was a narrow single track structure and was the location of the sea lock. It weighed in the vicinity of 250 tons and lasted for over 60 years. The trees on the centre left of the photograph formed part of the Grove Estate, and were removed in the late 1880s for development to commence. The thatched building in the centre of the photograph is the Ice House, used for the storage and distribution of imported ice.

The narrowness of the bridge is well illustrated in this very old print.

Another excellent view of the first swing bridge, together with an mixed assortment of shipping.

The South Pier and Reading Room in 1870, with vessels at anchor off the South Beach. Note the splendid beach where the present yacht club has a clubhouse and car park.

Construction of the second swing bridge is well advanced in this 1890s scene, as a paddle tug brings a trader through the channel from the Inner Harbour. The tug will probably take the vessel to just outside the harbour entrance.

The second swing bridge shortly after opening with ancillary work still being carried out. The previous narrow single track bridge can be seen alongside.

The South Pier was a popular centre of entertainment in the 1920s, with bands, concert parties, variety, and novelty acts. Crowds of people can be seen on the bandstand jetty, adjacent to the pavilion and bandstand, and on the pavilion verandas. It is possible that one of the regular band concerts is in progress. Lowestoft certainly knew how to entertain the vast number of visitors that came to the town for their holidays.

4417. — HARBOUR AND ENTRANCE TO SOUTH PIER, LOWESTOFT

THE PALACE, LOWESTOFT

The town lost many theatres and cinemas in latter part of the 20th century. One of these was the *Palace,* seen in this postcard by Lowestoft publisher A. Crisp & Son. The majority of the land on which the *Palace* stood has become a road and car park. The building was opposite the Royal Plain.

4418 - SOUTH BEACH & PROMENADE, LOWESTOFT

The south beach at Lowestoft in 1922, as seen from the Claremont Pier. The large prominent building on the left, comprised of two dwellings known as *Blenheim* and *Apsley*. For many years from 1921, these were used for work in connection with fishery research. This historic building, as with many others seen in this photograph along the Esplanade, has since been demolished. A once familiar feature on the the sands, and noticeable in this fine view, are the small boats used for making short pleasure trips off the beach.

A 1920s early morning view looking south, from the fishery research building mentioned in the previous caption. The Claremont Pier can be seen on the left, and with no traffic on the road, and only a small number of pedestrians, it is an idyllic scene. An interesting added attraction are the illuminated flower beds and lawns, lit by hundreds of decorative lights in the Wellington Gardens.

Wellington Gardens, Lowestoft.

London Road, Lowestoft

A bustling London Road South is portrayed in this postcard from 1904. A fine range of services, trades and shops were available in this well kept tidy traffic free environment.

At one time, F. W. Woolworth & Co. Ltd. had one of their many branches opposite the now demolished *Grand* cinema. The *Grand* can be seen to the left of the large telegraph pole in the centre of the photograph.

London Road South, Lowestoft.

Another view of a vibrant London Road South in Kirkley, with its wide range of shops. The Post Office is on the left with the butchers on one side, and on the other, a branch of the well-known local fruiter and greengrocer Dorlings.

41

Opened in July 1893, the *Grand Hotel* was a highly rated establishment. Built on the cliffs at Pakefield, it commanding superb sea views. A noted feature was the *American Bar*, regarded by many as East Anglia's finest ballroom.

During the early 1930 a dance hall was added on the north side of the hotel. This dance hall, known as the *Palais de Danse*, was to outlive the hotel by many years, not closing until the 1960s, whereas the hotel never reopened after the Second World War. The commanding position it had, is well illustrated in this view looking south from outside the newly completed Kensington Gardens in the 1920s. The building now forms part of the large fishery research complex, having been purchased by the Government in 1953. The town has been associated with this type of work since 1902.

In 1922, the Kensington Gardens were created at a cost of around £10,000. The work was carried out as part of a work creation scheme. Seen here is the water feature, not long after the Gardens were completed.

Looking north from Pakefield cliffs towards Lowestoft on a fine summers day in the early 20th century. This scene would change drastically in future years due to the relentless power of the sea. Many deckchairs are to be seen on the beach, but not one is in use. Perhaps the occupants did not wish to have their photograph taken!

Pakefield Beach

PAKEFIELD CLIFFS. LOOKING SOUTH. 1929.   SPASHETT'S SPECIAL PHOTOS.

Spectacular erosion of the cliffs occurred at Pakefield, and it was not until the 1930s that the cliffs were stabilised. The erosion affected a number of roads, and had a major effect on property in the area.
This card is from the well-known Spashett series, and possibly sold from their shop in London Road North, during the late 1920s. It shows houses either being left to their fate at the mercy of wind and tide, or being dismantled, the materials being recovered for further use. It is typical of what happened in Pakefield for many years.

Top Right-Many properties in Pakefield Street were lost when they fell down the cliff face or were demolished, because they were destined to fall. This applied to a number of buildings seen in this finely detailed postcard, published in the village around 1909 by R. M. Wood of Church Road.

Bottom Right – A good illustration of the early and unsuccessful attempts to protect the cliffs from the sea.

Below - The work connected with construction of the Jubilee Wall and also stabilisation of the cliff face, was mainly carried out in the mid 1930s. But some work, as seen here, was carried out in the 1940s. Just visible are two lorries depositing material down the cliff face and property awaiting the demolition men.

PAKEFIELD STREET.

6891

Pakefield, in the Year 1906, Since Fallen into the Sea owing to the Coast Erosion No. 635

The *Cliff Hotel* on the right of this scene recorded in 1903, would soon disappear as it became yet another casualty of the disappearing Pakefield coastline.

Pakefield, in the Year 1903, which has since fallen into the Sea owing to the coast erosion   No. 653

Despite the problems on the cliffs, life went on. This scene is from before the First World War, and shows a horse and cart belonging to a coal merchant standing outside the *Tramway Hotel*. An open top tram awaits departure from the Pakefield terminus for the journey north. Apart from a few single deck cars, the majority were of the type seen here.

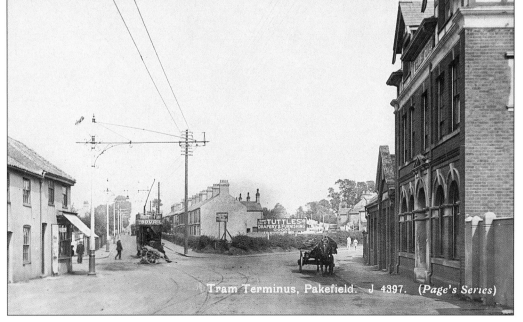

Tram Terminus, Pakefield.   J 4397.   (*Page's Series*)

Looking south from the terminus in 1933, we find a quiet, peaceful and traffic free London Road. The owner of the splendid Austin motor car, is apparently shopping in one of the many trading establishments which made Pakefield such a pleasant place to shop.

A view along what we now know as Stradbroke Road, in the days when it was known as Carlton Road. The traffic free road is unmade, and no pavements exist.

The Ship Inn, Carlton Road, Pakefield.   J 4381.   (Page's Series.)

Pakefield is well known for the long established holiday centre, which is situated between the main A12 trunk road and the cliffs. It is presently part of the Pontins chain of holiday centres. For many years it was known as Pakefield Hall Holiday Camp, and it is from that period, that this view of the southern part of this large site originates Just visible is the lighthouse tower, this was originally built at Corton. It was later moved to Kessingland and eventually to Pakefield. Disused for many years, it now serves as a look out tower for the voluntary Coastwatch organisation.

Normanston House and the associated land came into the possession of the town in 1924. A large and fine building, the house was later demolished. The land made a spacious and extensive open area, running down towards Leathes Ham and Lake Lothing. In recent years a section of the park has been used for the construction of a road. This postcard was published in the early 1930s.

The *Lady of the Lake* public house is prominent in this early view of Bridge Road, Oulton Broad. The buildings on the left, are opposite to the yacht station. These precede the former Waller's supermarket and restaurant which for so many years were part of Oulton Broad, and are now divided into small shop units.

A detailed postcard from the early 1900s with Bridge Road in Oulton Broad still unmade at that time, containing a wide range of shops supplying a variety of services. On the corner with the tobacconist, are the celebrated village haircutting, shaving and shampoo rooms.

With ladies chatting in the middle of the unmade road, Bridge Road looks a truly charming and peaceful location. This scene was recorded in the years just before the First World War. The grocer on the corner of Commodore Road with the cart outside, is seen to sell a wire variety of goods. This postcard is from the "Sunny Oulton" Series, published in the village by Chas E. Field of the Broadview Studio.

A peaceful scene from the late 1920s with a fine range of wooden pleasure craft awaiting customers. Work commenced on building the *Wherry Hotel*, seen in the background on the left, in 1899. It replaced an earlier hotel of the same name, at the same location. The railway swing bridge seen on the extreme right of the photograph was built in 1903. This replaced the earlier one, constructed in 1859. The building of this railway from Lowestoft to Ipswich, gave the town a direct route to London. This enabled fast expresses to travel from London to Lowestoft in just two hours 36 minutes. These expresses all included a luxury buffet or restaurant car.

The *Royal Hotel* is prominent in this view from the South Pier Pavilion, in the early years of the 20th century. This hotel was built in 1849 as part of Sir Morton Peto's plan for development of the area south of the bridge. During 1852, the building was enlarged by the adding of an upper storey. Wonderful views could be obtained from the hotel, which became one of the most highly rated establishments on the east coast. It had extensive private grounds with many amenities. The *Royal* was demolished in 1973, having been disused for some time. The land on which the hotel stood, remained vacant for many years. Eventually in 1993, part of the site was used for the construction of the East Coast Pavilion. The *Royal Hotel* coat of arms, removed during the demolition of the building can be seen in the Pavilion. The spire to the right of the *Royal Hotel*, is that of St. John's Church. This was built 1853-54, also as part of Peto's development plan and demolished in 1978.

View from the Pavilion, Lowestoft.

Sparrow's Nest, Lowestoft

An early 1900s view of the Sparrow's Nest, the story of which is told on page 15 of this book. This building, originally the seaside home of Mr. Sparrow, was extensively altered and extended during the Second World War.

Empire Hotel
Lowestoft

Built on Kirkley Cliff, the 200 bedroom, *Empire Hotel* opened in 1900. However, as a hotel, the large building was to have quite a short life, and by the early 1920s it had become *St. Luke's Hospital*. One of a number of large buildings in the town used for military purposes during the Second World War, it was demolished in 1958, having stood disused since the war. The site is now occupied by a school and playing field. The *Empire* is seen here shortly after opening.

Christmas Greetings

LOWESTOFT NEW PIER FROM CLIFF

Sent with Christmas Greetings, this 1905 postcard shows the Claremont Pier with a Belle steamer in attendance.

Construction by the Coast Development Company of the 670 foot Claremont Pier was completed in May 1903. This shows the pier in the 1930s with the new pavilion built on the pier after the initial opening. The landing stage can be seen on the extreme right of the picture. For many years the public have not been allowed on the pier because of its deteriorating condition.

Commencing in 1897, the Belle paddle steamers, owned by the Coast Development Company, ran regular return services in the summer months from London to Great Yarmouth. En route these steamers stopped at various places including Lowestoft, where they dropped off and picked up passengers from the end of the Claremont Pier. One of these steamers is seen lying at the Claremont Pier. This vessel is believed to be the *Yarmouth Belle*, built in 1898 at Dumbarton. Other "Belles" to operate the service included the *Southend Belle* and *Walton Belle*.

A high quality print, taken from an original glass negative, showing the Esplanade before the Claremont Pier had been built. From the late 19th century, this print shows a wealth of detail, including a paddle tug and a smack leaving the harbour, the South Pier and pavilion, a very busy beach and many bathing machines, some displaying a soap advertisement. The hand capstans required to pull the bathing machines up the beach can clearly be seen.

Lowestoft Pier Pavilion.

Badges, logos and images make interesting additions to postcards as in the case of this view of the South Pier Pavilion and Children's Corner. The logo representing Lowestoft is based on the old Borough seal, which was used for civic purposes until about 1914. This postcard dates from the early 1900s.

The setting sun over the Waveney Dock makes a colourful scene as the sailing trawler *LT 415 Ethel May,* passes the steam drifter *LT890 Doris*.

A splendid sight for visitors and locals alike, as three Lowestoft sailing trawlers leave port for the fishing grounds. Vessels such as these were working from the port until the Second World War. The nearest vessel is the converter smack *LT622 Ruby*, built in 1894, she became *YH975* in 1907, and was sold to Norway in 1912.

With a band and a tram following, and crowds watching, an army unit makes it's way up London Road South during the early years of the 20th century. Many will remember the shop on the right of this photograph as Woods, a popular bread and cake shop.

LOWESTOFT VOLUNTEER TRAINING CORPS

C METCALF
LOWESTOFT

A further scene from the early 1900s showing the Lowestoft Volunteer Training Corps marching along an unmade St. Peter's Street.

This scene may give the impression that it is an example of a topic we hear much about, that of global warming and rising sea levels. In fact it is a view of the south beach with a particularly high tide in 1905. In the background, the tower of the *Empire Hotel* can be seen, and to the left of that, the *Grand Hotel*.

Another scene from the early 1900s, in this case, there appears to be insufficient water! However, the occupants of the large tented camps on the denes appear to be getting the situation under control with beaters, and a bucket chain organised. The cliffs are adjacent to Gunton Cliff Esplanade, for long referred to as the Lowestoft Cliffs.

An excellent view, from just before the First World War, of the refreshment pavilion, bandstand and weather monitoring station in Belle Vue Park. The Royal Naval Patrol Service Memorial, now stands at this location.

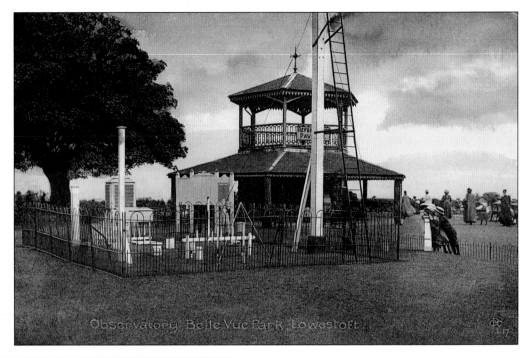

The South Pier Pavilion which was built in 1891 and demolished in 1954, was replaced by another, which opened in May 1956. The new building was in effect an entertainment centre. It comprised two dance floors, restaurants and bars, a theatre and a glass tower, referred to as the "Space Tower". From the top of this, superb views could be obtained in all directions. The pavilion was demolished early in 1989. It is seen here together with the yacht basin, in 1982. Outside the pavilion can be seen a number of children's amusements.

As already mentioned, the town has lost many places of entertainment, with dance halls, theatres and cinemas closing for a number of of reasons. The much loved Sparrow's Nest Theatre was one such building. Here we see the building, which in wartime meant so much to members of the Royal Naval Patrol Service, and in peacetime was a popular place of entertainment for visitors and locals alike. In this 1991 view it is being demolished.

Making way for the W. H. Smith store and a shopping arcade, the partially demolished remains of the *Odeon* cinema, present a sad sight for the thousands of patrons who remember it as a large first class centre of entertainment. A great many in the town wonder why this imposing and magnificent building with its many artistic murals, beautiful surroundings and the luxurious one thousand eight hundred and seventy two seats was destroyed. It could rival any cinema in the land. The *Odeon* was equally able to stage live shows as well as top rating films. For children, the Saturday morning shows were very popular with large queues forming outside. The young people were eager to get in, and see their favourites such as Laurel and Hardy, Charlie Chaplin, Tweety and Sylvester, Flash Gordon, Buck Jones, Batman, Roy Rogers and the Lone Ranger on the screen.

During the Second World War, Lowestoft was very much in the front line. One of a great many properties to be damaged or destroyed was the London Road North store of F. W. Woolworth & Co. It was destroyed in 1941. This scene shows a military ceremony, complete with band, being held on the site of the store, after the rubble had been cleared away. A prominent notice advising shoppers that the Woolworth store in Kirkley, was open, can be seen.

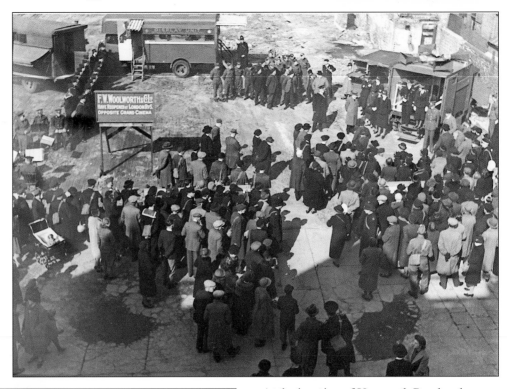

At the junction of Yarmouth Road and North Parade in June 1923, we find a splendid carnival float passing, with the participants wearing a fine assortment of hats. Apparently the float, indicating the support of the local Carnival Committee for Great Yarmouth, was heading for Yarmouth to participate in their carnival procession. The lorry appears to be an AEC Y-Type, one of many purchased by the local bus operator and builder United Automobile Services from the government, for later conversion to what were known as "lorry buses". The United took over the bus services of the Great Eastern Railway in 1913, and after becoming a major force in passenger road transport, were themselves taken over in 1929. The United was the forerunner of the Lowestoft based Eastern Coach Works, a major bus and coach builder.

Bus and coach building by Eastern Coach Works and the preceding companies, made Lowestoft famous. Throughout the British Isles and abroad, the many thousands of vehicles built in Lowestoft displayed the town's name for all to see, on the internal builder's plate. The construction of bus bodies at Lowestoft commenced in the early 1920s. A major blow to the town occurred when it was announced that the Coach Works was closing. In 1987, the last bus built at Lowestoft left the factory, to join the London Transport fleet. A local institution died.

Right - A completed Bristol type LS bus stands outside the front of the factory, proudly displaying the Eastern Coach Works poster. Buses and coaches left the factory displaying these, as they made their way to operators throughout the country and abroad. This particular vehicle would soon be heading for Wales, to join the fleet of Red & White, a company with headquarters in Chepstow.

A newly arrived bus chassis stands outside the factory. These were a familiar sight being driven through Lowestoft and Oulton Broad, as they made their way to the Coach Works, from far away places such as Bristol.

Another great local industry which was instrumental in making the name of Lowestoft widely known throughout the world, was shipbuilding. As with bus and coach building, shipbuilding is no longer a feature of the local scene. The last major shipyard to close, in 1994, was that of Richards (Shipbuilders) Ltd., and it is at that yard that these photographs were taken. The other large local well-known shipbuilder in recent times, Brooke Marine, closed in 1987. However, under a new company, Brooke Yachts, the yard survived until 1993.

Right - All is set for a new Royal Navy minesweeper to be named and then enter the water. The launching party, watched by many spectators, is assembled ready for the big moment.

Below - A few minutes after being launched on the 20th March 1984, the cargo vessel *Pamela Everard* is seen being manoeuvred by tugs. This photograph was taken from on board a minesweeper, then under construction at the yard.

Two food processing and canning factories, Morton's and the Cooperative Wholesale Society (CWS), were for many years local landmarks, and through their products, the name of Lowestoft became famous around the world. Morton's was situated on Horn Hill and the CWS on Waveney Drive. They both provided permanent large scale and seasonal employment. Morton's was set up in Lowestoft in 1901 and closed in 1988, the factory chimney being destroyed by explosive expert "Blaster" Bates in 1991. Morton's produced a vast range of goods, not all of which were canned products. The origins of the CWS factory in South Lowestoft can be traced back to around 1890, when the Maconochie Brothers moved their existing food production plant from Raglan Street to the site. The CWS took over around 1920, and it was later sold to Barber Richmore. The factory closed in late 1997 and was demolished in 2000. Both these factories are seen above, Morton's on the left with the CWS factory, seen here on the right.

PHOTOGRAPHIC INDEX

BACK COVER PHOTOGRAPHS

Top Left

During the 20th century, the area around the bridge, Royal Plain and the South Pier became a focal point in the town. This is the scene, in the early 1900s, from the Royal Hotel looking across the Royal Plain and the South Pier. The Pavilion on the pier was completed in 1891, and was demolished in the spring of 1954.

Top Right

In 1929, Mr. Howard Hollingsworth gave the 12.9 acres of land in Oulton Broad, comprising Nicholas Everitt Park, to the Borough of Lowestoft. Henry Everitt, known as Nicholas, lived for the latter part of his life in Broad House in the park. He planned to set up sports facilities for use by local people in the park, but died before his plans were implemented. His great friend, Mr. Howard Hollingsworth, purchased the park, carried out Everitt's plans to the full, and then presented, with conditions, the park to the town. This postcard shows the Broad before the park was given to the town. The second Wherry Hotel can be seen across the water, with industrial premises on the extreme left of this scene. A small steam launch can be seen on the right.

Bottom Left

A view of the Inner Harbour during in the early 1900s.

Bottom Right

Bathing machines on the south beach. The first such machine was introduced at Lowestoft in 1768, the design being copied from bathing machines in use at Margate.